CRAFTY
Stamping

Petra Boase

Gareth Stevens Publishing
A WORLD ALMANAC EDUCATION GROUP COMPANY

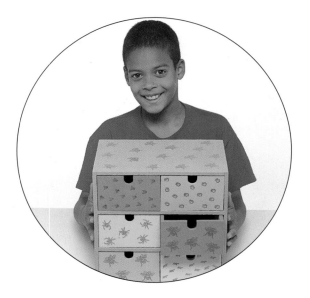

For Biba

The original publishers would like to thank the following children, and their parents, for modeling for this book: Kristina Chase, Lana Green, Leoni Hughes-Brown, Lee Johnson, Reece Johnson, Janel Kiamil, Mai-Anh Peterson, Alexandra Richards, and Leigh Richards.

Thanks also to the following manufacturers for providing the rubber stamps and other materials for this book: First Class Stamps (fish, *pages 16-17, 34-35*; seaweed, *pages 34-35*; flowers, *pages 40-41, 44-45*; doodles, *pages 54-55*). Inca Stamp (paw print, *pages 14-15*; shell, *pages 16-17*; pig, chicken, *pages 22-23*; globe, *pages 24-25*; sunflower, *pages 26-27*; octopus, shell, group of shells, *pages 34-35*; bumblebee, *pages 52-53*). Make Your Mark (dalmatian, *pages 18-19*; rocket, *pages 24-25;* dragon, pig, *pages 38-39*; butterfly, *pages 60-61*). Rubber Stampede (Scottie dog roller, *pages 14-15*; cow roller, *pages 28-29*; watermelon, strawberry, *pages 30-31, 36-37, 46-47*; bug, *pages 42-43, 52-53*; motifs, *pages 48-49*; butterfly, *pages 50-51*; chili pepper, cactus, *pages 56-57*).

The author would like to thank Lisa Edwardes for her help in the studio.

For a free color catalog describing Gareth Stevens' list of high-quality books and multimedia programs, call 1-800-542-2595 (USA) or 1-800-461-9120 (Canada). Gareth Stevens Publishing's Fax: (414) 225-0377.

Library of Congress Cataloging-in-Publication Data

Boase, Petra.
    Crafty stamping / by Petra Boase.
        p. cm. — (Crafty kids)
    Includes bibliographical references and index.
    Summary: Tells how to use store-bought rubber stamps or ones you make yourself to decorate all kinds of items, including wrapping paper, folders, stationery, gift bags, shoelaces, and more.
    ISBN 0-8368-2503-9 (lib. bdg.)
    1. Rubber stamp printing—Juvenile literature. [1. Rubber stamp printing. 2. Handicraft.] I. Title. II. Series.
TT867.B63   2000
761—dc21   99-42734

This North American edition first published in 2000 by **Gareth Stevens Publishing**
A World Almanac Education Group Company
1555 North RiverCenter Drive, Suite 201
Milwaukee, WI 53212 USA

Original edition © 1996 by Anness Publishing Limited. First published in 1996 by Lorenz Books, an imprint of Anness Publishing Limited, New York, New York. This U.S. edition © 2000 by Gareth Stevens, Inc. Additional end matter © 2000 by Gareth Stevens, Inc.

Senior editor: Caroline Beattie
Photographer: John Freeman
Designers: Tony Sambrook and Edward Kinsey
Gareth Stevens series editor: Dorothy L. Gibbs
Editorial assistant: Diane Laska-Swanke

Printed in Mexico

1 2 3 4 5 6 7 8 9 04 03 02 01 00

Introduction

Stamping is a creative form of decoration — and it is great fun! If you are unable to buy ready-made rubber stamps, you can make your own stamps out of materials you probably have at home.

The projects in this book are exciting. After reading only a few of them, you might already want to start working. Before you do, however, you must organize your work space and materials. Be sure to cover the surface on which you will be working with newspaper or an old, clean cloth, and have all the equipment you will need close by.

Whether you use ready-made rubber stamps or homemade stamps, remember to wash each stamp gently after use and before you switch to a different ink color. After washing, carefully dry stamps with an old towel. Also remember to keep the lids on the printing inks. If you forget to cover them, they will dry out. The most important thing about stamping is to let your imagination run wild and have lots and lots of fun!

Petra Boase

Contents

Materials and Equipment

Fabric ink pens

Fabric paints

Pigment ink pads

FABRIC INK PENS AND FELT-TIP PRINTING PENS

Fabric ink pens and felt-tip printing pens look a lot alike, and they are used the same way. You ink a stamp by coloring it with the pen. Then you press the stamp onto fabric (if you are using a fabric ink pen) or paper or cardboard (if you are using a felt-tip printing pen). You can use several pens of different colors on a single stamp. Remember to cover these pens after each use to keep the ink from drying out.

PIGMENT INK PADS

These stamp pads are made with a stronger ink than most others, and the colors are very bright. You can use this ink for stamping on wood, as well as on paper or cardboard.

FABRIC STAMP PAD

You can pour any color stamping ink onto a fabric stamp pad, but you will need a separate pad for each color. When the ink runs out, just pour on some more.

RAINBOW INK PADS

These stamp pads have several colors of ink on a single pad. When you print a stamp with it, the figure or design will be multicolored.

WOODEN BLOCK STAMPS

The heaviest stamps generally are those mounted on wooden blocks, but even these stamps come in a variety of sizes. This kind of stamp feels very stable when you print with it.

RUBBER STAMP KIT

Probably the cheapest way to buy rubber stamps is in a kit. A kit often has a theme, such as bugs, flowers, or sea life, and you usually get lots of different individual stamps in the kit.

STAMPS WITH HANDLES

Having a handle on a stamp helps you get a firmer hold on the stamp when you are making a print. As a result, figures and designs print more clearly and evenly.

FABRIC PAINTS

These paints are specially made for use on cloth, rather than on paper, cardboard, or wood. When applied to fabrics, this paint will not wash out.

GLITTER GLUE

This bottled mixture of glue and glitter is great for decorating stamp prints. Be sure to let the glue dry thoroughly, or the ink will smudge.

Stamps with handles

Square ink pads

Felt-tip printing pens

Glitter glue

Roller stamps

Rainbow ink pads

Cat's-eye ink pads

Wooden block stamps

Rubber stamp kit

Fabric stamp pad

Ink pads

INK PADS

Stamp pads, with ink already on them, can be purchased at stores that sell art and craft supplies. They come in many colors, shapes, and sizes. Some are for printing only on paper and cardboard; others contain fabric ink for printing on cloth. Cat's-eye and square ink pads are named for their shapes. Because of their size, they work best with small rubber stamps.

ROLLER STAMPS

A long rubber stamp that is mounted on a roller will print a continuous line of the stamp's design or motif. First you roll the stamp on an ink pad, then you roll it over the surface on which you want to print. The longer you want the line of designs to be, the more ink you will have to apply to the stamp. Using a roller stamp might take some practice.

STAMPING INK

Ink that can be used for stamping generally comes in a bottle and is available in a variety of colors. (Be sure to use fabric ink for stamping onto cloth.) Pour the ink onto a fabric stamp pad to use it. Some inks come with roll-on or brush-on applicators. Replace the lid on the bottle after each use and screw it on tightly to prevent messy leaks or spills.

Creative Ideas

Rubber stamps come in many shapes and sizes and in an incredible variety of figures and patterns. You can create interesting special effects by using different colors, designs, and techniques.

1 Use a roller stamp to decorate a ribbon for wrapping a gift or to put in your hair.

2 Try to get the same effect as a roller stamp by using an ordinary stamp to print a figure or a design several times in a row.

3 Repeat a figure or a design several times in neat rows to create an orderly pattern.

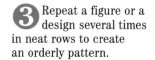

4 Repeat a figure or a design in a scattered arrangement to create a more unusual pattern.

6 Closely match ink and paper colors to create a subtle print.

7 Use sharply contrasting ink and paper colors for very bright results.

5 Experiment with different color combinations of ink and paper. Pink ink on blue paper, for example, makes a purple print, whereas blue ink on pink paper still makes a blue print.

Homemade Stamps

Making your own stamps means you can create your own unique designs.

STRING

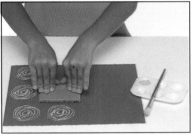

1 String will make a design with nice fine lines. Cut out a square of thick cardboard and brush glue over it. Starting in the center of the square, coil string into a spiral. Cut the end of the string when the spiral is the right size.

2 When the glue is dry, coat the string with paint (use fabric paint for printing onto cloth). Press the stamp firmly to make a print. You will have to reapply paint to the string for each print.

CORD

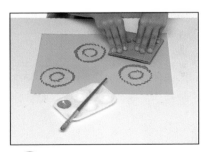

1 Cord will make a design with a chunky, textured effect. Cut out a square of thick cardboard. Then cut a piece of cord and glue it in a circle on the cardboard. Cut a shorter piece of cord and glue it in a smaller circle in the center of the first circle.

2 When the glue is dry, coat the cord with paint (use fabric paint for printing onto cloth). Press the stamp firmly to make a print. You will have to reapply paint to the cord for each print, but, to keep the design clear, do not use too much paint.

CARDBOARD

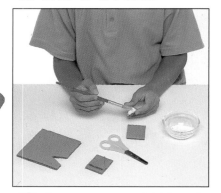

1 Cut out a square of thick cardboard. Then cut another piece of cardboard into any shape you want and glue it onto the square. Let the glue dry completely.

2 Press the stamp facedown on a pigment ink pad (use a fabric ink pad for printing onto cloth). To make a print with the stamp, press firmly and reapply ink for each print.

ERASER

1 Draw a shape onto one side of an eraser. Ask an adult to cut away the eraser from around the shape with a craft knife.

2 Press the stamp facedown on an ink pad, then make a print. An eraser will give your stamp a smooth finish, like store-bought rubber stamps.

SPONGE

 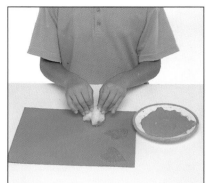 

1 Sponge stamps add texture to a design. Draw a shape on a sponge with a felt-tip pen. Ask an adult to cut away the sponge from around the shape with a craft knife.

2 Pour paint onto a plate (use fabric paint for printing onto cloth). Dip the stamp into the paint, then make a print. Wash the sponge when you have finished printing.

POTATO

1 Cut a potato in half. On one half, draw a shape with a felt-tip pen. Ask an adult to cut away the potato from around the shape.

2 Press the stamp facedown on an ink pad, then make a print. If you are printing onto cloth, remember to use a fabric ink pad.

Creating a Picture

You can create a picture with stamps in several ways. Print combinations of figures and designs to build a scene. Repeat a stamp to form a pattern. Give the same stamp many looks, using different coloring techniques.

1 Use a variety of stamps and colors to create a picture or a scene. The picture below is about sea life. You could even write a story to go with the scene you create.

2 A pattern of repeated images can be either very compact, like these bones, or spread out. You can also experiment, making patterns with more than one image.

3 To make sure you are stamping in a straight line, first draw a guideline with a ruler and a pencil. Print your stamps along this guideline. When the stamp prints are dry, erase all the pencil marks.

4 You will be amazed at how many different effects you can get with one stamp. For a very colorful effect, print the same figure or motif in different colored inks on different colored pieces of paper. Then cut out the images and arrange them on cardboard.

5 Stamp a figure or a design on paper using pigment ink. When the ink is dry, carefully apply glitter glue over parts of the image. Allow the glitter glue to dry thoroughly.

6 When you use pigment ink by itself, pick colors you really like. Choose the color of the paper carefully, too. Experiment with different ink and paper colors to create your favorite combinations.

7 A rainbow ink pad makes a single stamp print in several colors at the same time. When using rainbow ink, be sure all the colors will show up on the paper you choose.

8 You can color parts of a stamp with fabric ink pens or felt-tip printing pens. In this example, the stamp was colored with red and green pens before printing; the black seeds were colored in later.

Paw Print Paper

Create your own designer wrapping paper to make gifts for family and friends look extra special. You can make matching ribbons, too!

YOU WILL NEED
- Colored paper
- Paw print stamp
- Pigment ink pads
- Scissors
- Ribbon
- Tape
- Scottie dog roller stamp

1 Lay a large piece of colored paper on a smooth, flat surface. Stamp the paper with paw prints, arranged either in rows or in a random pattern.

2 Cut a piece of ribbon long enough to wrap around your package. Lay the strip of ribbon on a flat surface. Smooth out the ribbon and tape down both ends.

3 Roll the Scottie dog stamp over an ink pad, then carefully roll it along the ribbon. To cover a long piece of ribbon, you will need to re-ink the stamp. Try to match up the design each time you re-ink.

4 When the ink is dry on both the paper and the ribbon, you are ready to wrap! Finish off the package with a pretty patterned bow.

Fishy Folders

Give an ordinary ring binder or a file folder a new look with a fishy front. Adding a pocket to the cover of the binder will give you a convenient place to store pens and pencils or a small notepad.

YOU WILL NEED

- Scissors
- Colored cardboard and paper
- Ring binder
- Glue and glue brush
- Fringe
- Fish stamps
- Pigment ink pads
- File folder
- Shell stamp

1 Cut a piece of colored cardboard into a rectangle smaller than the cover of the ring binder. Brush glue along both long sides and one short side of the rectangle and attach it to the front of the binder, with the unglued edge at the top.

2 Cut a piece of fringe to fit along the top edge of the pocket and glue the fringe in place. You can make your own fringe by cutting deep slits, that are all the same length, along one edge of a strip of paper.

3 Draw lots of fish shapes on colored paper and cut them out. Print fish stamps on the paper fish with pigment ink. When the ink is dry, glue the paper fish onto the binder and the pocket.

4 Also glue some of the paper fish onto a file folder. Print shells around the fish to create a sea life motif.

17

Pom-pom Pencil Pot

Transform a plastic soft-drink bottle into
a container for anything from pencils
to wooden spoons.
If you have lots of
plastic bottles, you
can make a set of
containers, covering
each one with a
different color
of paper.

YOU WILL NEED

- Plastic bottle
- Tape measure
- Craft knife
- Heavy paper
- Scissors
- Dalmatian stamp
- Pigment ink pad
- Double-sided tape
- Pom-pom braid
- Glue and glue brush

1 Draw a line around a plastic
bottle at the same height all
the way around. Ask an adult to
cut the bottle for you, along that
line. Keep the bottom half of the
bottle and recycle the top half.
Measure the height of the bottle,
then measure around the bottle.

2 Cut a piece of heavy paper with
height and width measurements
that match the measurements of the
bottle. Add ¼ inch (½ centimeter) to
the width for overlap. Lay the paper
on a smooth, flat surface and print
dalmatian stamps all over it. Let the
ink dry thoroughly.

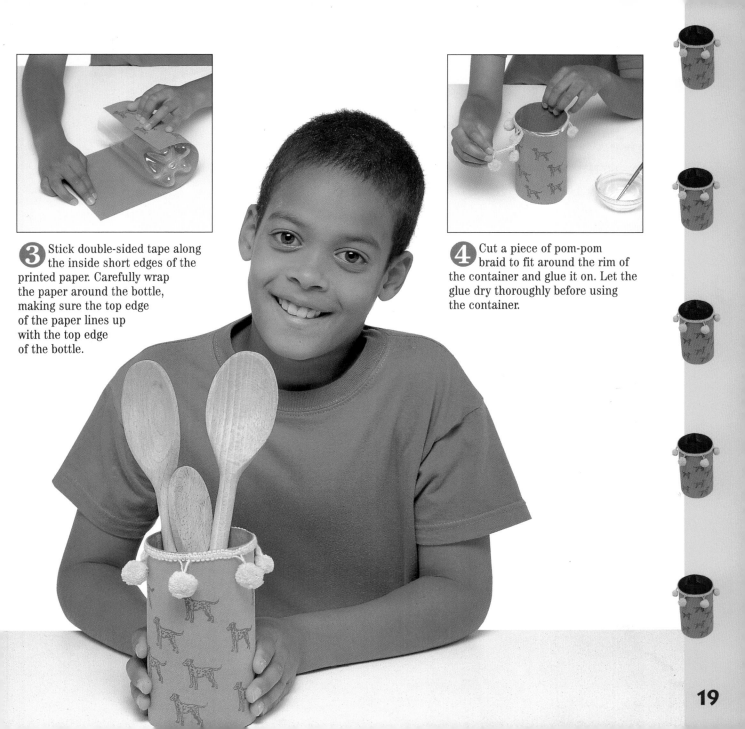

3 Stick double-sided tape along the inside short edges of the printed paper. Carefully wrap the paper around the bottle, making sure the top edge of the paper lines up with the top edge of the bottle.

4 Cut a piece of pom-pom braid to fit around the rim of the container and glue it on. Let the glue dry thoroughly before using the container.

19

Starry Pillowcase

Use your stamping skills for textile printing and design your own pillowcase. If you are very ambitious, why not decorate sheets to match the pillowcase?

YOU WILL NEED
- Sponge
- Felt-tip pen
- Craft knife
- Heavy paper or cardboard
- Plain pillowcase
- Fabric paint
- Paper plate
- Iron
- Paper towels

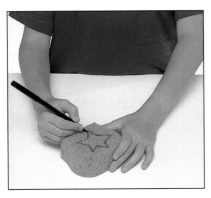

1 Draw a star on a smooth sponge with a felt-tip pen.

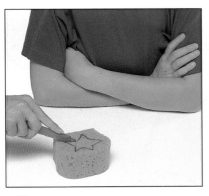

2 Ask an adult to cut around the star with a craft knife.

3 Put heavy paper or cardboard inside a pillowcase and lay the pillowcase on a smooth, flat surface. Pour fabric paint onto a paper plate and dip the sponge star into it. Press the star gently onto the pillowcase to make a print. Dip the sponge into the paint for each print.

4 When you finish stamping the first side of the pillowcase, let the paint dry thoroughly. Then turn over the pillowcase and stamp the other side. When the pillowcase is finished, and the paint is completely dry, ask an adult to iron over the star prints to make the paint show up better. Cover the prints with paper towels before ironing. The paper towels will keep the paint from sticking to the bottom of the iron.

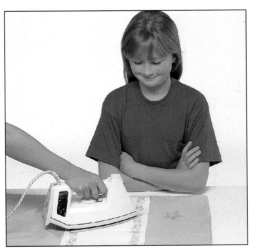

21

Covered Boxes

Recycle cardboard boxes by jazzing them up with decorated paper. These boxes are terrific for storing odds and ends of all kinds. Empty shoe boxes are perfect for this project.

YOU WILL NEED
- Scissors
- Colored paper
- Pig stamp
- Chicken stamp
- Pigment ink pads
- Cardboard boxes
- Glue and glue brush

1 Cut out paper circles in lots of bright colors. Make the circles by drawing around the top of a glass or the lid of a jar with a pencil.

2 Stamp each circle with pig or chicken prints, using brightly colored inks that contrast with the colors of the paper.

3 When the ink is completely dry, decorate a box, one side at a time, arranging the circles where you want them before gluing them on.

4 You might want to cover the box completely, with a contrasting color of paper, before gluing on the circles. You can also cover a box completely with colored paper, then stamp figures and designs all over the paper, instead of onto paper circles.

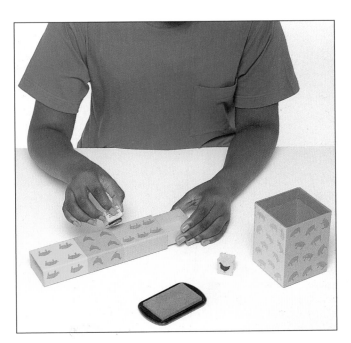

Lovely Letters

Your friends will enjoy reading a letter from you even more when it comes to them on stylish designer writing paper you have made yourself. Matching envelopes with decorative seals will make all the mail you send first class!

YOU WILL NEED
- Envelope
- Colored paper
- Scissors
- Glue and glue brush
- Rocket stamp
- Pigment ink pads
- Cat's-eye ink pads
- Globe stamp
- White self-adhesive stickers

1 If you are not sure how to make an envelope, simply take one that has not been used and open the seams. Place the opened envelope on a piece of colored paper and draw around it. Cut along this outline, then, using the envelope as a guide, fold the colored paper in the right places. Glue the sides to hold the envelope together, but leave the top flap open.

2 Cut a piece of colored paper, making it almost as wide as the envelope and twice as long. Lay this piece of paper on a smooth, flat surface and stamp a decorative border around the edges. Stamp the front of the envelope with the same design, if you want to. Let the ink dry thoroughly before you start writing a letter.

3 Use cat's-eye ink pads to color a globe stamp, then make a print of the stamp on a plain white, self-adhesive sticker. You will need to re-ink the globe stamp for each print you make.

4 When the ink is dry, cut around the globe. After you have written a letter, put it inside the envelope. Then use the globe sticker to seal the envelope.

HANDY HINT

You can make designer notepaper, too! Just stamp an identical figure or motif on each page of a notepad. You must work slowly and carefully, however, to make sure that the pages of the notepad do not tear off and that the ink on each page is completely dry before lifting the page to stamp the next one.

Flower Cards and Tags

Homemade cards or gift tags on presents to friends and family members add a delightful personal touch. Why not make matching wrapping paper, too? Just stamp the same design you print on a card or a tag onto a piece of colored paper.

YOU WILL NEED
- Sunflower stamp
- Pigment ink pads
- Colored paper
- Scissors
- Colored cardboard
- Hole punch
- Glue and glue brush
- Ribbon

1 Stamp a sunflower onto several pieces of colored paper. You can use a variety of paper and ink colors, but remember to wash the stamp after using each color of ink. Cut out the sunflowers.

2 To make a gift tag, cut a piece of colored cardboard into the shape of a tag, such as a luggage tag, (as shown above) and punch a hole at the tapered end with a hole punch. Glue a sunflower onto the tag.

3 To make a greeting card, fold a piece of colored paper in half and glue a sunflower onto the front. Be creative by making your cards and gift tags in as many different ways as possible.

4 You can either glue or tie tags onto gifts. To tie on a gift tag, you need to add a ribbon. First, fold a piece of ribbon in half, then push the folded end through the hole in the tag, and, finally, pull the loose ends of the ribbon through the loop at the folded end.

27

Fringed Party Cups

Make your next party more fun with these
clever and colorful drinking cups!

YOU WILL NEED

- Ruler
- Scissors
- Colored paper
- Plastic or paper cups
- Cow roller stamp
- Pigment ink pads
- Double-sided tape

1 Measure and cut out a strip of colored paper 2 inches (5 cm) deep and long enough to fit around the top of a plastic or paper cup.

2 Roll the cow stamp, first, over an ink pad, then, along one edge of the paper strip. Let the ink dry thoroughly.

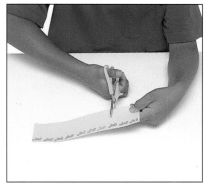

3 Fringe the opposite edge of the paper strip by making evenly spaced cuts, all the same length, into it. Do not cut into the stamp prints.

4 Stick a strip of double-sided tape along the back of the uncut edge of the paper strip, behind the row of cows. Then carefully stick the paper fringe around the top of the cup, about ½ inch (1.3 cm) below the rim. You might need a friend to hold the cup steady while you attach the fringe.

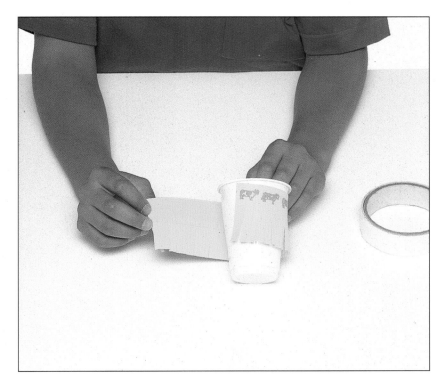

Fruity Shirt and Shorts

This outfit is perfect for a summer day, when the Sun is shining and the weather is warm. Your friends will be impressed — so you should not be surprised when they ask where you bought it.

YOU WILL NEED
- T-shirt
- Paper or cardboard
- Fabric ink
- Fabric stamp pad
- Strawberry stamp
- Watermelon stamp
- Shorts
- Iron
- Paper towels

1 Lay a T-shirt out flat on a covered work surface. Put a piece of paper or cardboard inside it to keep the ink from soaking through to the other side of the shirt.

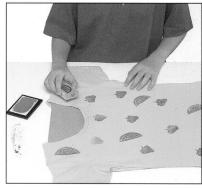

2 Pour fabric ink onto a fabric stamp pad. Stamp strawberries all over the front of the T-shirt, then stamp watermelons between the strawberries.

3 Lay a pair of shorts out flat on your work surface and put paper or cardboard inside the legs. Stamp a border of strawberries across the leg openings. Remember to re-ink the stamp before each print.

4 When the ink is completely dry on both the T-shirt and the shorts, ask an adult to iron them for you, to set the ink. To protect the bottom of the iron, cover the prints with paper towels before ironing over them.

Polka-dot Pillowcase

Add some color to a plain pillowcase by painting lots of polka dots on it. Then print another color over the polka dots with a homemade potato stamp.

YOU WILL NEED
- Potato
- Knife
- Felt-tip pen
- Newspaper
- Pillowcase
- Fabric paints
- Paintbrush
- Stamping inks
- Fabric stamp pads
- Iron
- Paper towels

1 Ask an adult to cut a potato in half. With a felt-tip pen, draw a circle on one half of the potato. Then have an adult cut away the potato from around the circle, so the circle is raised.

2 Cover a work surface with newspaper and lay a pillow-case out flat on it. Put another piece of newspaper inside the pillowcase to separate the two sides. Paint large circles on one side. Let the paint dry thoroughly.

3 Ink the potato stamp on a fabric stamp pad and make a print on one of the painted circles. Stamp a potato print on each circle. For variety, use several colors of ink.

4 When the ink is completely dry, ask an adult to iron over the polka dots to set the paint and the ink. Cover the polka dots with paper towels to protect the bottom of the iron.

33

Sea Frieze

Decorate a wall with this magical frieze of colorful sea life. If you have the right stamps, your scene can even include a deep sea diver — or sunken treasure!

YOU WILL NEED
- Glue and glue brush
- Squares of colored paper
- Large piece of cardboard
- Pigment ink pads
- Shell stamps
- Seaweed stamps
- Fish stamps
- Octopus stamp

1. Glue squares of colored paper, side by side, along the bottom of a large piece of cardboard. Make sure all of the squares line up evenly because you will be stamping prints over the seams where the edges of the colored squares meet.

2. Use pigment ink pads in several colors to stamp your prints. Try some of the creative ideas for using color described on page 8. Start by stamping shell prints along the bottom of the squares. Remember to stamp some prints over the seams.

3. Now stamp seaweed prints along the squares, above the shells. Step back to look at the frieze, now and then, to see how your work is progressing and to make sure you are stamping the various prints in the right places.

4 Finally, stamp the fish and octopus prints in the open spaces around the seaweed and shell prints. Stamp any other sea life figures you might have in places appropriate for your scene. Be sure to let all of the prints dry thoroughly.

Gift Bag

This little bag is an attractive way to present a gift. You can make a bigger bag for a larger gift but be sure the gift is not so heavy that it breaks the bag.

YOU WILL NEED
- Ruler
- Scissors
- Colored and white paper
- Glue and glue brush
- Hole punch
- Ribbon
- Felt-tip printing pens
- Strawberry stamp

1 Measure and cut out a piece of colored paper 12 inches (30.5 cm) by 5½ inches (14 cm). Fold the paper in half, then unfold it again. Fold over ¼ inch (½ cm) on each long side.

2 Brush glue along the folded edges. Then fold the paper in half again, pressing firmly along the glued edges so they will stick together. Let the glue dry thoroughly before you start decorating the bag.

3 Punch two holes, at least 2 inches (5 cm) apart, through the top of the bag. Thread an 8-inch (20-cm) piece of ribbon through the set of punched holes on each side of the bag. Tie knots at the ends to hold the ribbons in place.

4 Use felt-tip printing pens to ink the strawberry stamp, coloring the leaves green and the strawberry red. Stamp strawberry prints onto a piece of white paper. You will have to re-ink the stamp for each print. Then cut out the strawberries and glue them onto a square of colored paper. Glue this square onto the bag.

HANDY HINT

Instead of making your own bag out of colored paper, you can recycle a small paper bag. Then all you have to do is punch holes at the top, attach the ribbon, and decorate the bag. You might also try using cord or twine, instead of ribbon — for a more natural look!

Party Napkins

Decorate a party table with your own designer napkins. Have even more fun by stamping each napkin with a different figure, or in a different pattern, for each of your party guests.

YOU WILL NEED
- Plain colored paper napkins
- Scissors
- Pigment ink pads
- Dragon stamp
- Pig stamp
- Star stamp

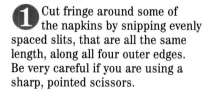

1 Cut fringe around some of the napkins by snipping evenly spaced slits, that are all the same length, along all four outer edges. Be very careful if you are using a sharp, pointed scissors.

2 On some of the other napkins cut zigzag spikes or curvy scallops around the edges. Make sure that all the spikes and scallops are evenly spaced.

3 One at a time, unfold each napkin, lay it out flat on a smooth surface, and stamp on a border of prints. Use any figure or pattern you like, but keep the stamp prints lined up and evenly spaced.

4 Decorate inside the border with more stamp prints, using different figures. Let the ink on the napkins dry thoroughly before you refold them and place them on the party table.

Flower Power Leggings

Give a pair of plain leggings some fashion power by stamping them with lots of flowers. You can use fabric ink colors that blend in with the leggings or try contrasting colors that, perhaps, match a T-shirt.

YOU WILL NEED

- Clean paper
- Plain colored leggings
- Scissors
- Fabric ink pads
- Flower stamps
- Leaf stamp
- Iron
- Paper towels

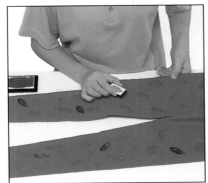

1 Cover your work surface with clean paper and lay a pair of leggings out flat on it. Cut pieces of paper to fit each leg and the top of the leggings and put these pieces inside the leggings.

2 Using a fabric ink pad, stamp flower prints all over the leggings. Stamp the flowers close together. The leggings will stretch when you wear them, so the flowers will spread out a little.

3 Use a fabric ink pad in a contrasting color to stamp leaf prints between the flowers. Allow plenty of time for the ink to dry thoroughly before you turn over the leggings to stamp the other side.

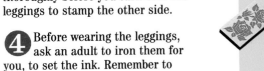

4 Before wearing the leggings, ask an adult to iron them for you, to set the ink. Remember to cover the prints with paper towels to protect the bottom of the iron.

41

Spider Socks

Shock your friends with these creepy-crawly socks. Use socks made of cotton so they can be ironed to set the ink.

YOU WILL NEED
- Plain colored cotton socks
- Fabric ink pads
- Spider and bug stamps
- Iron
- Paper towels

1 Lay the socks flat on a protected work surface. Using a fabric ink pad, stamp spiders onto the socks.

2 Then stamp smaller bugs around the spiders, using a different color of ink. When the ink is completely dry, turn the socks over and stamp the other sides.

3 If you stamp the same pattern on two socks that are different colors, you can wear those two odd socks together!

4 When the stamp prints are completely dry, ask an adult to iron each sock (with paper towels covering the prints) to set the ink — so the bugs will not crawl off!

Blossoming Lamp Shade

For bedtime reading fun, decorate the shade of your bedside lamp with blossoms. Large felt blooms with small flower prints stamped between them make a nice variety.

YOU WILL NEED
- Pen
- Felt
- Scissors
- Glue and glue brush
- Lamp shade
- Flower stamp
- Fabric ink pads
- Latex paints
- Paintbrush

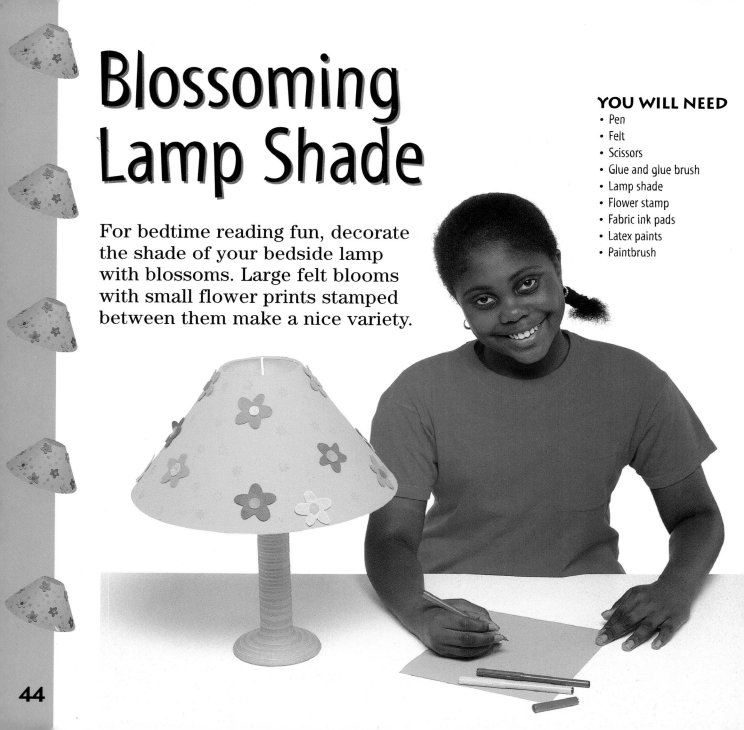

1 Draw flower shapes on pieces of felt and cut them out. Then cut out felt circles in contrasting colors for the centers and glue them onto the flowers.

2 Glue the felt flowers onto a lamp shade. Press on a flower with one hand while holding the back of the lamp shade, behind the flower, with the other hand.

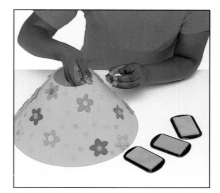

3 Gently stamp flower prints between the felt flowers, using fabric ink pads in a variety of colors. As you stamp, support the back of the lamp shade with your free hand.

4 You could also paint the base of the lamp in either a bright color, to match some of the flowers, or a pattern, such as stripes. Let the base dry thoroughly before you attach the lamp shade to it. Ask an adult to screw in a lightbulb for you. Then plug in the lamp and turn it on!

HANDY HINT

Be very gentle when you are stamping the flower prints onto the lamp shade. The shade is not very firm, and you do not want to risk smudging your design.

Melon Basket

If you think this watermelon wastebasket looks too good to use for trash, why not store things in it, instead?

YOU WILL NEED
- Watermelon stamp
- Colored paper
- Pigment ink pads
- Scissors
- Paintbrush and paints
- Plain square wastebasket
- Glue and glue brush
- Homemade star stamp

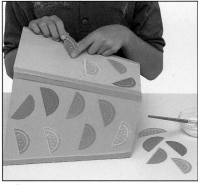

1 Stamp watermelon prints onto pieces of paper using a variety of paper and ink colors. Remember to clean the stamp before using a different color of ink.

2 When the ink is dry, cut out the watermelons.

3 Paint the wastebasket all one color, then paint the corner edges a contrasting color. When the paint is dry, glue the watermelons to the outside of the wastebasket.

4 Use an eraser to make your own star stamp (see page 10). Then stamp the inside of the wastebasket with star prints.

Stamped Scarf

Wear this decorative scarf around your neck or in your hair. You can easily make a scarf to decorate. Simply cut out a square piece of plain fabric and hem the sides by folding over the edges and sewing them down.

YOU WILL NEED

- Large white scarf or square piece of white fabric
- Assorted rubber stamps
- Fabric ink pads
- Clean cloth
- Iron

1 Spread a scarf out flat on a protected work surface. Stamp the same figure or design, in the same color of ink, onto the four corners of the scarf.

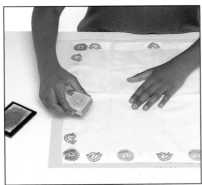

2 Using fabric ink pads in a variety of colors, stamp different figures or designs around the edges of the scarf.

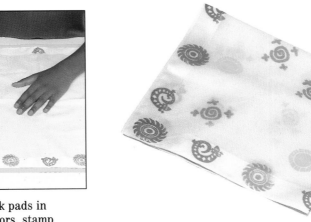

3 Stamp more prints, in various colors, onto the middle of the scarf. Let all of the stamp prints dry thoroughly.

4 Then cover an ironing board with a piece of clean cloth. Place the scarf facedown on top of the cloth. Ask an adult to iron the scarf for you to set the inks.

5 When you choose the ink colors for your stamp prints, try to match them to colors in your wardrobe, so you can wear your new scarf with some clothes you already have.

Butterfly Pencil Case

You can make a nifty pencil case out of brightly colored felt. If you do not like to sew, you can use fabric glue to hold the sides of the case together and Velcro, instead of snaps, to fasten it.

YOU WILL NEED
- Large square of felt
- Needle
- Thread
- Fabric glue and glue brush
- Snaps
- Scraps of felt
- Butterfly stamp
- Fabric ink pad
- Scissors

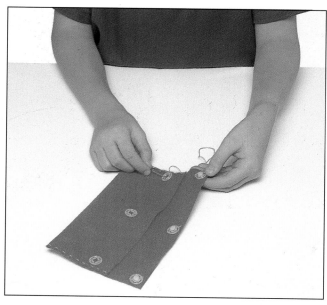

1 Fold a square of felt as shown in the picture above. Sew each side closed or carefully glue the side edges together with fabric glue.

2 Sew on three snaps, positioned (as shown, right) with one side of the snap underneath the top flap of the pencil case and the other directly opposite on the facing piece of felt.

3 On each of three scraps of felt, each scrap a different color, stamp a butterfly print. When the prints are completely dry, cut out the felt butterflies.

4 Glue the butterflies, one over each snap, on the outside of the flap on the pencil case. The butterflies will hide the stitching for the snaps.

Bug Drawers

If you have an old cabinet or a small piece of furniture, why not give it a fresh coat of paint and decorate it with stamp prints? Remember that painting is messy, so cover your work surface with lots of newspaper or an old cloth.

YOU WILL NEED
- Small chest of drawers
- Latex paints
- Paintbrush
- Pigment ink pads
- Set of bug stamps
- Bumblebee stamp

1 Before painting a chest of drawers, you must remove the drawers from the frame. Paint the frame a bright color and let the paint dry thoroughly. You might need two coats of paint.

2 While the frame is drying, paint each drawer separately, using several different colors of paint.

3 When all of the paint is dry, put the drawers back into the frame. Use pigment ink pads to stamp a different group of bug prints onto the front of each drawer.

4 Stamp bumblebee prints on all sides of the frame. Be sure the ink on all of the stamp prints is completely dry before you put anything into the drawers.

HANDY HINT

Be sure to use latex paint for this project. Fresh latex paint cleans up easily with water, so you will not need any dangerous chemical paint thinners or removers, such as mineral spirits or turpentine.

53

Sneaker Doodles

Give a pair of sneakers an exciting new look by doodling all over them and dotting them with glitter. For an extra splash of color, replace their plain shoelaces with brightly colored ribbons.

YOU WILL NEED
- White canvas sneakers
- Newspaper
- Set of doodle stamps
- Fabric inks
- Fabric stamp pads
- Fabric glitter glue
- Ribbons

1 Stuff each sneaker with crumpled newspaper, pushing the paper in snugly to make the canvas firmer and easier to stamp prints on.

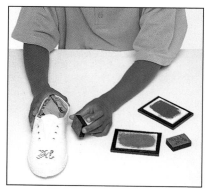

2 Stamp doodle prints onto the sneakers, pressing very gently. It might help to slip one hand inside the shoe, holding it behind the spot where you will stamp.

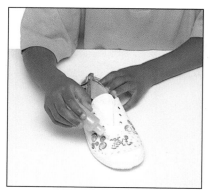

3 When the doodle prints are completely dry, decorate around them with squiggles and dots of fabric glitter glue. Allow plenty of time for the glitter glue to dry.

54

4 As a finishing touch, thread a piece of brightly colored ribbon through the lace holes of each shoe. Then just put on your sneakers — you are ready to dance!

55

Cactus Dish Towel

This dish towel is guaranteed to spice up any kitchen — and it makes a great gift.

YOU WILL NEED

- Plain dish towel
- Cactus stamps
- Fabric inks
- Fabric stamp pads
- Chili pepper stamp
- Iron
- Clean cloth

56

1 Lay a dish towel out flat on a covered work surface. Stamp one kind of cactus around the edges, leaving about a 4-inch (10-cm) gap between each print.

2 Stamp a different kind of cactus, in a different color, between the first set of cactus prints, all the way around the towel.

3 Cover the middle of the dish towel with chili pepper prints, using bright red fabric ink. Let the ink prints dry thoroughly.

4 To set the ink prints so they will not easily wash out, ask an adult to iron over them for you. Before ironing, lay a clean piece of cloth over the ironing board. Then lay the dish towel, with the design facedown, on the cloth.

Deco Duffel

This project will give you some practice making your own stamp out of cord (see page 9). You can use your deco duffel for laundry or for sports equipment or even as a travel bag.

YOU WILL NEED
- Thick cardboard
- Scissors
- Cotton cord
- Glue and glue brush
- Pillowcase
- Needle
- Thread
- Clean paper
- Fabric paint
- Paintbrush
- Ribbon
- Safety pin

1 Cut out a square of thick cardboard. Then cut a piece of cord and glue it in a circle on the cardboard. Cut a shorter piece of cord and glue it in a smaller circle in the center of the first circle. Cut a small strip of cardboard and fold it in half. Brush glue on one half and press it onto the back of your homemade cord stamp to form a handle.

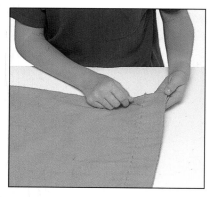

2 Fold over the open end of a pillowcase, about 2 inches (5 cm), and sew it down to form a kind of tunnel all the way around the opening of the pillowcase. If you do not know how to sew very well, ask an adult to help you.

3 Lay the pillowcase out flat on a smooth, covered surface and put a piece of paper inside to keep the front and back separated. Brush fabric paint over the cord stamp, then press the stamp down firmly on the pillowcase to make a print. Cover one side of the pillowcase with prints, reapplying paint to the cord stamp for each print. When the paint is dry, stamp the other side.

4 Cut a strip of ribbon three times the width of the pillowcase and attach a safety pin to one end of it. Snip a hole in the tunnel around the opening of the pillowcase and thread the ribbon through it, using the pin to move the ribbon along. When the ribbon gets back to the opening, take off the pin and tie the ends of the ribbon together. Pull the ribbon to close the bag.

Flowery Frame

Put a favorite photograph of a friend or a pet — or a special piece of your artwork — in this fun frame and hang it on your bedroom wall.

1 Draw an 8-inch (20-cm) square on heavy cardboard or poster-board. Then draw a 3-inch (7.5-cm) square in the center of the large square and ask an adult to cut out both squares with a craft knife.

2 Draw flowers on colored paper, using as many different colors as you like, and cut them out. Also cut out circles in many colors for the centers of the flowers. Glue the circles onto the flowers.

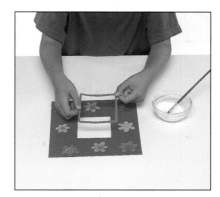

3 Glue the flowers onto the card-board frame. Ask an adult to cut a thin frame out of colored paper to fit around the hole in the center of the cardboard frame. Carefully glue the paper frame in place.

4 Using a pigment ink pad, stamp butterfly prints between the flowers, all around the frame. Let the ink dry thoroughly before you turn the frame over to add a backing and a hanging loop.

5 Have an adult cut out a 4-inch (10-cm) square of cardboard. Tape it to the back of the frame, over the opening. Tape only the bottom and side edges, leaving the top open to slip in a photo. To make a loop for hanging the frame, cut a short piece of ribbon, fold it in half, and tape it to the top edge of the frame.

Glossary

coil: (v) to wind something in a spiral or a series of rings around itself, starting at a center point.

contrasting: showing a distinct, or even opposite, difference when being compared.

dalmatian: a type of medium-size dog that has short white hair with black or brown spots on it.

deco: short for *art deco*, a popular style of modern art that can be recognized by its bold geometric shapes and zigzagged lines.

doodle: (v) to scribble absentmindedly or sketch random designs, shapes, and figures that have no real purpose.

duffel: a large cloth bag, often used in camping, sports, and travel, to carry clothing, laundry, and other personal items.

frieze: a decorative strip of sculptured or painted figures, scenes, or designs trimming the walls of a building, either inside or outside, or bordering the ceiling of a room or the roof of a building.

fringe: (n) threads, strands, or strips of material hanging loosely from some kind of edging to form a decorative border.

image: a picture or some other kind of visible representation of a person or an object.

ink: (v) to coat, color, or cover with ink.

latex paints: paints that have a water, rather than oil, base.

motif: a repeated design or idea, usually related to a theme, in a work of art.

pigment: a substance that provides color when it is mixed with a liquid, such as the powder added to paint to produce a particular color; in nature, a substance in the cells and tissues of plants and animals that provides their color.

random: made or done by chance, without planning or arrangement.

scallops: a series of semicircular-shaped curves forming a decorative edge.

smudge: (v) to brush or rub into a blur, streak, or smear.

tapered: wider at one end and gradually narrowing toward a slimmer opposite end.

textile: cloth, or fabric, made by weaving or knitting threads, yarn, or fibers.

texture: the look or feel of fabric or some other kind of material due to the way its threads or fibers are interwoven.

thread: (v) to pass material through a hole or an opening that is usually small or narrow.

wardrobe: all of the clothing that belongs to an individual at any given time.

zigzag: a series of, usually, short lines connected in a way that forms sharp angles and turns pointing, alternately, in opposite directions.

More Books To Read

The Art of Rubber Stamping. Michele Abel (Creative Impression)

Build Your Own Bugs. Build Your Own Dinosaurs. Books and Rubber Stamp Kits. Dennis Schatz (Andrews McMeel)

Craft Works Rubber Stamping. (Silver Dolphin)

Fabric. Craft Workshop (series). Monica Stoppleman and Carol Crowe (Crabtree)

Make Cards! Art and Activities for Kids (series). Kim Solga (North Light Books)

The Metropolitan Museum of Art: Fun With Pattern. Fifi Weinert (Viking Children's Books)

The Official Smokey Bear Book and Stamp Kit. (Ladybird Books)

Printing. Arts and Crafts Skills (series). Susan Niner Janes (Children's Press)

Rubber Stamp Art: Funstation. Susan Niner Janes (Price Stern Sloan)

Stamping Made Easy. Made Easy (series). Martin and Susan Penny, editors (Sterling Publications)

Videos

Donna's Day — Art Surprises. (Tapeworm Video)

Make a Print. Kids 'n' Crafts (series). (Morris Video)

Relief Printing. Art Smart (series). (Crystal Productions)

Web Sites

members.aol.com/Letterboxr/carving.html/

www.delta.edu/~sehatter/index.html

Due to the dynamic nature of the Internet, some web sites stay current longer than others. To find additional web sites, use a reliable search engine with one or more of the following keywords: *art, crafts, fabric painting, handicrafts, hobbies, printing, printmaking, rubber stamps,* and *stamping.*

Index